DOMESDAY BOOK

MANCHESTER
UNIVERSITY PRESS

THE CRITICAL IMAGE

This series explores the historical and contemporary uses of photography.
It aims to develop photographic history and criticism and investigates practice.
The publications draw on methods and theories widely used in art history, literature,
film and cultural studies.

Series editor John Taylor
Department of History of Art and Design
Manchester Metropolitan University

Already published

Jane Brettle and Sally Rice (eds) *Public bodies – private states: new views on photography,
representaion and gender*

Sarah Kember *Virtual anxiety: photography, new technologies and subjectivity*

John Roberts *The art of interruption: realism, photography and the everyday*

Lindsay Smith *The politics of focus: women, children and nineteenth-century photography*

John Taylor *A dream of England: landscape, photography and the tourist's imagination*

John Taylor *Body horror: photojournalism, catastrophe and war*

DOMESDAY BOOK

photopoem

Peter Kennard

MANCHESTER
UNIVERSITY PRESS

Manchester and New York

distributed exclusively in the USA by St. Martin's Press

Published by Manchester University Press
Oxford Road, Manchester M13 9NR, UK
and Room 400, 175 Fifth Avenue, NY 10010, USA
http://www.man.ac.uk/mup

Distributed exclusively in the USA by
St. Martins Press, Inc, 175 Fifth Avenue, New York, NY 10010, USA

Distributed exclusively in Canada by UBC Press, University of British Columbia, 6344 Memorial Road, Vancouver, BC, Canada V6T 1Z2

British Library Cataloguing-in-Publication Data
A catalogue record of this publication is available from the British Library

Library of Congress Cataloging-in-Publication Data applied for

ISBN 0 7190 5802 3 *hardback*
      0 7190 5803 1 *paperback*

First published 1999

06 05 04 03 02 01 00 99   10 9 8 7 6 5 4 3 2 1

Cover: photography by Jenny Matthews, photomontage by Peter Kennard
Designed by Peter Kennard and Peter Gladwin
Typeset in Avenir
Printed in Great Britain by The Pale Green Press, London

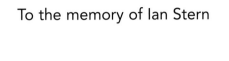

To the memory of Ian Stern

ACKNOWLEDGEMENTS

I am greatly indebted to the photographer Jenny Matthews, who took many of the photographs that are the basis for images in this book. Her encouragement, understanding and commitment to my work has been absolutely invaluable. Matthew Kennard has helped me put the words together from their tentative beginnings. Enormous thanks to him, and to Judy and Daniel, who put up with me and sustained me during the book's making. Great thanks to my editor Matthew Frost, and to John Taylor, for their belief in this book and their generosity and enthusiasm throughout its making. Great thanks also to the Pale Green Press, especially Peter Gladwin who has worked with me on a number of projects over twenty years, and whose understanding of my work and consequent ability to turn it into print is absolutely invaluable. I would like to express my sincere gratitude to Gimpel Fils, especially René Gimpel and Jackie Haliday, who have supported this project specifically, and over many years have shown great commitment to my work and given me enormous encouragement. I am very grateful to the Royal College of Art, especially Sarah Willcox, who has been incredibly helpful and supportive, as have Olivier Richon, Rachel Taylor and my other colleagues in Photography at the RCA. Thanks to Frank Thurston and Anders Kjaergaard for their photographic work on this book. Thanks also to Al Rees for the great discussions we have had over many years, and for pushing me on throughout the book's making. I would also like to thank: Anne Beech, Bryan Biggs, Sylvie Borel, Mohini Chandra, Alan Cooper, Bill Evans, Peter Hall, Mark Haworth-Booth, Amanda Hopkinson, Les Hutton, Maggie Lambert, Ken Livingstone MP, Peter Longfellow, Rab MacWilliam, Simon Meddings, Shirley Read, Peter Reading, Leo Stable, Chris Stewart, Doug Walla and Jan Woolf. I am grateful to the Arts and Humanities Research Board and the Royal College of Art for grants in support of this project. Finally, thanks to Harold Pinter for his very generous foreword. His work and commitment are an inspiration.

CONTENTS

FOREWORD

Kennard sees the skull beneath the skin all right: an area dominated by greed, indifference, ruthlessness, naked force against the powerless; the Holy Grail of the Big Buck. In *Domesday Book* he has woven a brilliant and ghastly tapestry about power, desolation, destruction, death and 'the market'. Word and image are locked together in a deadly and convulsive marriage. Kennard forces us to inhabit a grotesque and oppressive prison from which there seems to be no escape. The prisoner is the human spirit, chained, shackled, wasted, reduced, throttled.

Domesday Book is a stunning imaginative feat. The eyes of men, women and children which end the book are beautiful, tragic and unforgettable.

Harold Pinter

The off-cuts and rubble are closely packed in the disused workings. . .

The Stonemason, 3 January 1883

Domesday Book:

1

That night, with my carriers
Of clippings, photos, junk,
I pushed on

Under the river.
Walking a car tunnel,
I arrived at construction and mud.

That night I saw the foundations,
The pile of rubble,
The empty circle.

At every locked gate
An intruder alarm –
A click of light on auto-switch.

For every movement
A movement detector,
Photo-cells flashing – blind with light.

Pinned by a head-ache
Of clicks and flashes,
Skin lit through an X-ray of shudders,

Images flicked by in the planetarium
Thrown up
On the walls of my skull.

Dissolved in light –
My brain, a projector
Flashed back

Slides of unstoppable images,
Inverse
And terrible.

As if photos were hauled
Onto the scaffold
Of a century ticking under.

That night, the click, the flash,
My brain scared shitless
Flashed the century –

2

From rubble, a century's slip-way,
Exports emerge,
The dealers profit through the mud.

In my ears din
The same old voices,
Different throats.

From their gobs
The logo grin
Prevails.

Designed to omit
The export of arms
Designed to kill.

Wired for sound,
To give voice
To their voice,

Loud but deaf,
Dumb but loud.
Wired for power,

Broadcasting clichés of the vocal,
Designed for subtraction
And avoidance:

'Those removed, stay removed.
Those silent, stay silent.
Those classed 'under' stay under – '

In everyday war,
Fought by all means
Unnecessary.

This toxic celebration
Sees out the century,
Leaving the mute mute.

3

The city clicks –
My skull a pus-filled dome
Swimming in a century's slime.

Its roof is done for,
Leaking blood
On a thousand plinths.

Spewing and flashing,
Photos that oil the wheels
Into a menu for power

Slip and crash head-on
Into splinters
Of cause and effect.

Pictures merge and splash,
Torn limb from limb
They fuse and break.

A crush of photos
Folding into
The end of the century.

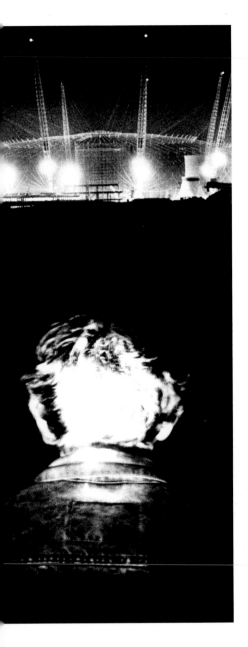
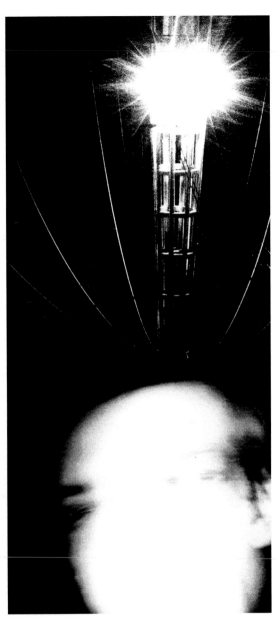

4

I reeled out from the circle
To the river's edge –
Where those who'd sheltered

Had been slung,
Then slung out.
The exclusion zone,

Too near the showcase,
The circle,
The news.

Light clicked on fluid and drift,
Plastic, cans,
Cardboard and sludge.

Newspapers that pillowed heads
Blew up,
Flicked by air:

Page 7, column 8 – *Famine*.
Page 19, columns 2 to 7 – *Ethics*.
Pages 22 to 38 – *'Another new high'*.

Located here, dislocated
Here and everywhere
Where two laws operate.

A place of rot, as ever
Bang on the edge
Of every show of office.

Shoved under the carpet
Badly laid,
Are migrant spoor,

'Ill-fitted' remains
Mapped out
In piss and vomit.

Imprinted through sweat,
Unsettled dust hugs
Skin

On pallets –
Faces,
Frozen in transit

Like boxes of flesh,
Fork-lifted onto pallets
Off the public shelves.

Contact printed
Autopsies
Of the bodies' emulsion.

'All isolated cases'
Forcibly removed
From the civic glare.

Eyes, ears etc.
Caked in blood,
Turin Shrouds of the written off.

5

I spin around the site
At the edge of discard,
Wood and card on sticks.

Rotting placards
Abandoned from an action,
Making a stand – now dust.

Flung away
To here, off centre,
A rim of history.

Or maybe fought off –
(Some smashed,
Some blood-spattered).

Slowed down remains,
Movement splintered
For archaeology.

Hands –
My hands?
Your hands?

Taut under pressure,
Miming the hands
Of the carrier,

Slither up sticks
Onto placards
Amputated into image.

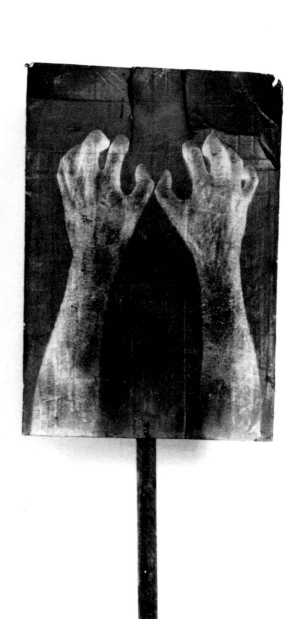

6

Neither there
Nor here,
My edges blown –

Heads, faces
Leak off bodies
Like unfixed film.

A reservoir of refuse
Builds up,
Bursts its banks.

Drowning hands grab pallets
Floating by
In congested filth,

Stopped short
In a crash
Of wood and limbs,

Beached
In the mud
Of millennial foundations.

From debris,
Dead centre
In the empty circle,

Punctured by light,
Pumping out images
From every cut,

A figure,
Dust grey,
Peels off a pallet.

Long coat, jeans,
Sodden carriers, junk,
Struggles to utter –

Gag off –
Takes voice –
Screams:

'O this –
Globe's wooden O
To this O.

A nil: by mouth,
By ear,
By eye,

By brain.
Seeing out the century
N.O.

Show our blankets
Caught on the wire.
Show a museum of the street.

Show the market shares
Profit in loss.
Show our nightly doorways on CCTV.

Show daily uprootings
A stone's throw from here.
Show eyes turning slowly – away.

Show knuckle-duster teeth,
Smiles glinting upriver,
Making a killing on free market screens.

Show that this virtual killing
Spills real blood.
It's a mouse-click from here,

Somewhere on a world map,
I don't know where. . .
Where it is.

But. . .
Show it
It is – '

Show:

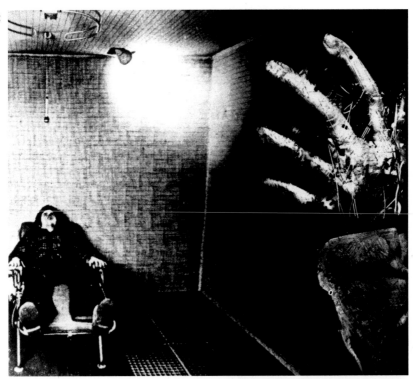

Show:

Show:

Show:

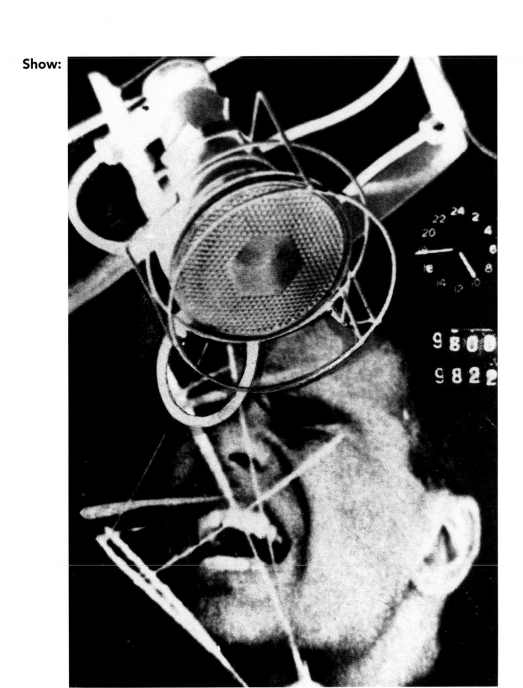

Show:

Show:

7

I wander through exhibits
Of the voice,
Here at the apex of past and future

Where a country so far
Is not gearing up
To scratch the surface,

Smoothed and polished
By sponsored spit
From the wizards of finance.

Voices echo, shadows switch off,
Criss cross my body,
Shadows switch on.

Each sudden beam
Flashes picture then sound
Then nothing –

Vision off – sound on.
Vision on – sound off.
The needle flickers:

Voice A
Exhibit B
Voice C

Exhibit D
Voice E
Exhibit –

Strobing
Between order
And question.

(Why) dig up
The shit
For the old old stories (?)

(Why) cut and paste
In the dissecting room
Of war and weapons (?)

(Why) excavate
For talking pictures,
Pictures that talk (?)

(Why) try and climb
A wall,
A wall of silence (?)

(Not) worth it. Worth it (?)
Last ditch scratchings
Against all knowledge:

'If you're picturing traces
Of history's lapse,
Kick over the traces – you

Keep your trap
Shut.
Design sugar cubes

For the tea cup,
Be blind
To the tea.'

Flick the damn switch –
Vision off.
Sound off.

8

In the hauntings
That flash,
Dark space

Clicks on and off
In random fits
And stops –

I stumble
On a wreck of tables,
Washed up,

Splintered,
Broken on the wheel
Of the monstrous circle.

Sitting at a table,
Its leg propped
On *Jane's Fighting Ships*,

I glue down cuttings
In a scrapped book
Of the century's exit.

Matters of fact, fleshed out
In a chaos of photos
Torn through and cut.

Seated around me,
Figures melt through figures,
Voices exchange larynx.

I am them
As flesh slides
Through flesh –

At the top table,
Set for celebration
In dead space

Are scattered treaties,
Statements, declarations,
Invoices, sanctions,

Spreadsheets, communiqués,
Export orders,
Edicts, dicta –

Smudged with mucus and grime.
Napkins
At an arms fair.

Spattered by dripping oil,
The greased papers
Become transparencies,

Windows
Of both surface
And depth.

In oil-doused vision,
I see words
And through words

Flesh opposed to words.
The action/inaction
Of a mirage of diners.

Embraced in the fetid cling
Of the arms
Of the arms dealer –

Banker winks
At General,
General winks

At Minister.
Minister shuts both eyes
Tight on 'collateral damage'.

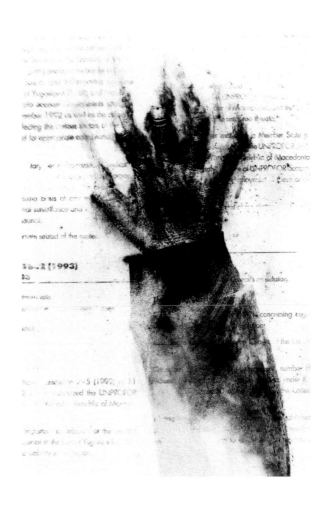

RESOLUTION 713 (19 ...

25 S ...ber 1991

Adopte ... imous vote.

...or ... Belgium, Fran... ...ub... the United ...

The Security ...

...cious of th... ...he convening of a Se... ...etter conveyed by the ... Yugoslavia to the Presid... (S/23069),

Having heard the sta... ...Yugoslavia

...

...ncerned that the continuation of the situa... ...ies a threat to international peace and secur...

Recalling ... responsibility und... the Char... ... international ...peace and se...

Recalling also the ...

... of a cease-fire including the ...
... convening of a Conference o... ...mechanisms set forth with... ...of all weapo...

...va... ...s e... ...and, in this co... ...er 1991 of th... ...n Security and ... ...gains or change ...dence are accept... ...cease-fire conclu... ...and also that si...

...ease fire ...

...ber 1991 to ...e Permanent ...

...ptember ...of the ...Rep...

United Nations high ... (UNHCR) and ... humanitarian ... ... of the International Conference on the Former Yugoslavia,

... rates its demands that all parties ... ... security of UNPROFOR, as well ... ... Nations personnel and the ... ... and ... ... out the Republic ...

... Council affirms ... ... upon the ... ... in the Republic ... ... and notes in ... ... civilian popul...

Welcoming also the cease-fire agreement between the Government of the Republic of Bosnia and Herzegovina ... the Bosnian Croat party, and the signature of the Washington framework agreements between the Government of the Republic of Bosnia and Herzegovina ... the Government of the Republic of Croat party, as steps towards ...

... importance of involving the Bosnian ... ... in an overall nego...

... signed on ... of Croatia and ... ... United Nations Pro... ... which was facilitated by the ... United States of America ...

... between the Republic ... ... Republic of Yugoslavia ... pursuant to the joint state ...

Welcoming ... significant progress achieved ... and **stressing** that ... ... UNPROFOR in the ... ... Bosnia and ... Croatia within the ... ... to consolidate ...

... President of the Security ... S/1994/... S/1994/1113 and ...

United Nations High Commissioner for Refugees (UNHCR) and other humanitarian organizations in reiterates its demands that all parties ensure the safety and security of UNPRO... as all other United Nations personnel... non-governmental organizations and their unimp... freedom of movement throughout the...

... Affirms its determination to maintain and ... the recent positive developments toward ... Republic of Bosnia and Herzegovina and ... no ... the importance ... and ... an pop ... confirming ... situation they ... examination of the report of the Secretary-General ... 1994/291) pursuant ... its resolution 900 (1994)...

RESOLUTION ... 31 March 1994

Adopted by un... vote ...

Prepared in the course of ... organizations ...

The Security Council...

Recalling ... relevant resolutions ... conflict in the territory of the former Yugoslavia and reaffirming in particular ... the mandate of the United Nations Protection Force (UNPROFOR)...

Having considered the reports of the Secretary-General of 11 March 1994 (S/1994/291), 16 M... 1994 (S/1994/300) and 24 March 1994 (S/1994/333 and Add. 1), and his letter of 30 M... 1994 (S/1994/367),

Having also considered the letter of the President of the Republic of Croatia d... March 1994 (S/1994/305),

... *emphasizing* the need for ... agreed settlement ... ed by all parties, and ... ming the continuing efforts of the Co-Chairmen of the Steering Committee

... of the International Conference on the Former Yugoslavia,

... the cease-fire agreement between the Government of the Republic of Bosnia and Herzegovina and the Bosnian ... and the signature of the Working ... agreement between the Government ... Republic of Bosnia and Herzegovina and ... Croatian ... party, as steps towards an overall settlement ...

Underlining ... efforts to achieve ... the Bosnian Serb party in ... to achieve a coverall ... personnel ...

... cease-fire agreement signed on ... between ... Republic of Croatia and ... Serb authorities in the United Nations Protected ... States of America ... Yugoslavia ... International Conference ... grave concern at the ... between the Republic ... Federal Republic of Yugoslavia ... pursuant to the joint state...

... the recent significant progress achieved in and around Sarajevo and **stressing** that a strong ... presence of UNPROFOR in this a... as well as in other areas of the Republic of Bosnia and Herzegovina and the Republic of Croatia ... framework ... mandate ... consolidate such ...

... the statement by the President of the Security Council of 14 March 1994 (S/PRST/...1994) ... Bosnia and Herzegovina ... 1994 (S/1994/300) and in this ... the recent developments ...

... bring about an end to the suffering of the civilian population in and around Maglaj.

...proposals on any...

...en to prevent this incident...

...personnel and allow the period... effect...

...sion, and ...tes him to submit such...

...urgent...

3. Calls ... on the Bosnian parties to agree to a...

sion of the ...ments on a cessation and a...

cessation of hostilities commencing ... and...

...ember 1994 beyond 30 April 19...

...ties and all others concerned... are...

...main seized of the matter.

Photograph this –
In the casinos
Of ordnance,

When a country's
Bombed off the map
Over there,

It's put
On the map
Over here.

Photos are trafficked
By dealers,
Stills are snapped up.

Smart hands are dealt
To brokers
Of smart bombs.

Uproot the artist's impression
And a flood of bodies
Covers the concrete.

From global debt,
Interminably signed
Dead cheques,

Dud babies,
Dud cheques,
Dead babies.

The nibs that sign
Are squashed and splayed
By bodies

Falling through the century.
Two lines of blotched ink,
Never meeting: going nowhere.

Needs asphyxiated by profit,
Land unpeopled
In conglomerate stink.

The centrifuge of power,
In an imperial glide,
Chucks out the grit.

The unsponsored voice
Is thrown to the edge
Of the audible.

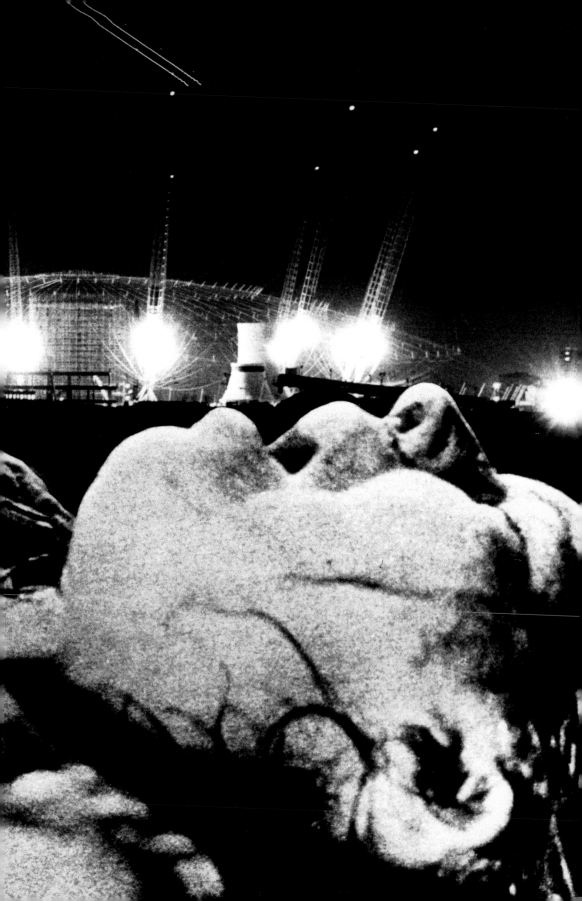

11

In the reek of oil,
Layered in sludge,
Cuttings ghost cuttings.

An encased bird,
Weighed down,
Drops to the circle.

The confident movements
Of buyers and sellers,
Bombed to the tables

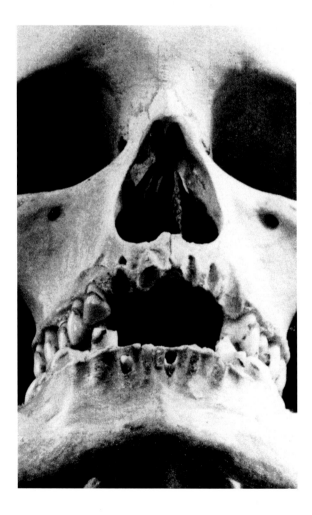

From market and alley,
Impacts in their gut.
Seizes up and concertinas

Into this buffer
Where the gravy train
Stops.

Crashing
Into my brain,
Searchlight rips –

Roams the wall
Of my skull
Glued up with pictures.

Skull an O
In an O
Of accelerated pixel.

The bird stops moving,
Grounded and glued
To a gravy of oiled earth.

Feathers stick
To old newspapers,
Eroded by footprints,

Torn through –
News reads with *Business*,
Business with *Arts*.

Scrambled, words lost,
Embedded in muck
Pages 2, 9, 32

Cut through
Saleroom Report
Page 10:

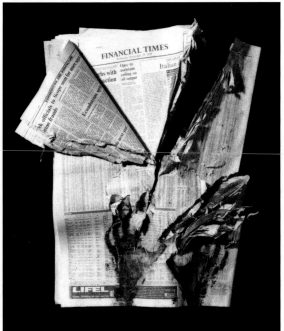

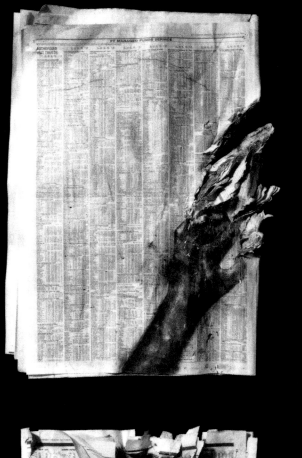

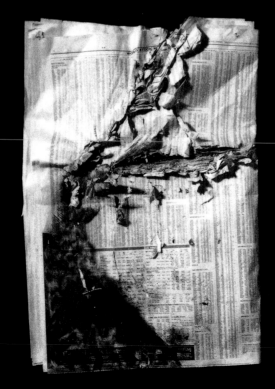

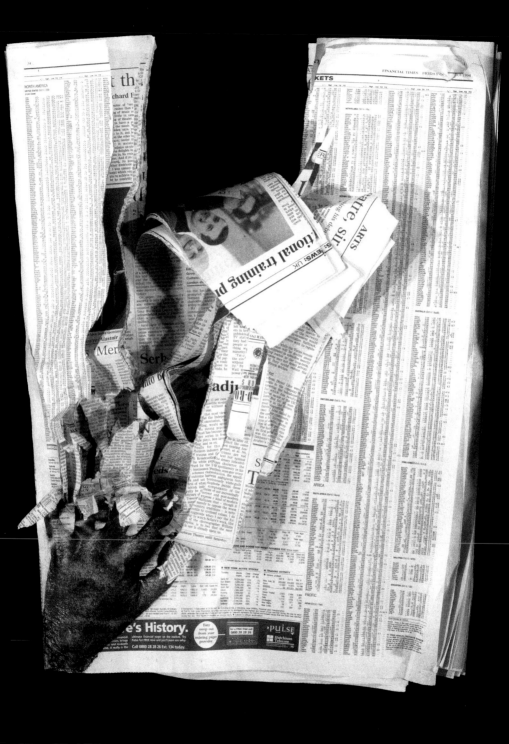

WORLD STOCK MARKETS

NORTH AMERICA

EUROPE

INDICES

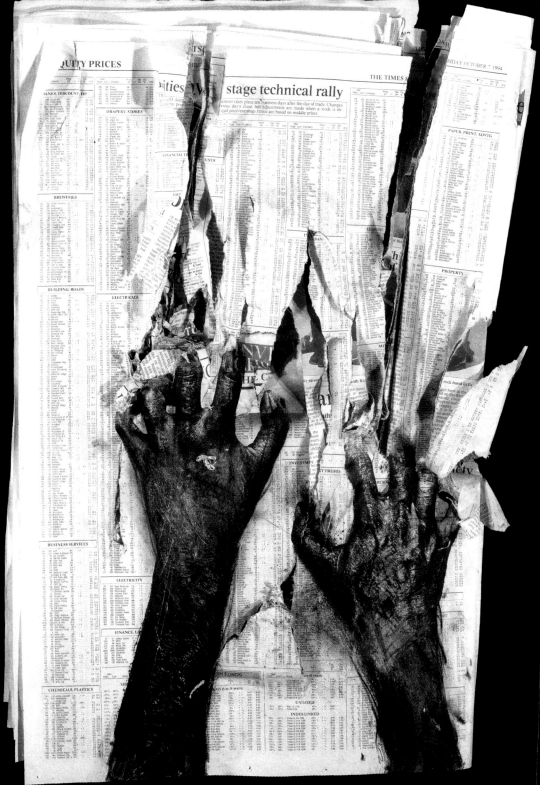

'LOT 1

In privat_ hands.
On loan fro_ public collecti__.
Conservation _eport, conditi__ beyond re____.

LOT _

North Ameri___ Sch_ol.
Contempor___.
To _ighest bidder.

Br_____ Aerosp___ Ground attac_.
_ollateral dama___ capac___.
Special _erms availa___.

____ _

Mach___ _uns.
Guarante__ _ill power.
Avail____ now (Gov_____ _ales agen__).

_OT _8

U.S/G.B ap_roved.
Long range strik_ capa____.
_or surgical strikes on _urgeries.

__T __1

_nti-person____ mine.
Invis____ fragm____.
Fo_ _____ use.'

Sick of forensics,
Verse flicks blank
Now –

In this –
A place
Where

Shrapnel
Is designed...
Designed.

Designed –
                –
Full stop.

12

I blank out –
Lyric ticks
Over on blanks.

Meter ticks off metre –
Say it
From scratch say:

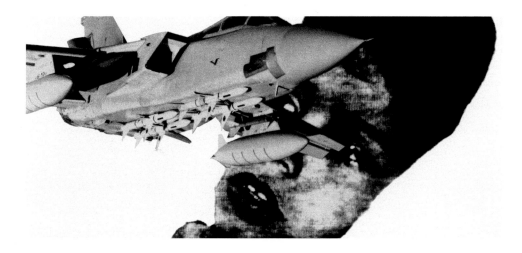

Say caption
As
Image: *The market rallies*

Say image
As
Caption:

FT 30 share down 24.4 at 2864.3	**Eurotop 300** down 18.18 at 1235.14
FTSE 250 up 5.6 at 4982.0	**Pound:** $1.6410; Euro: 1.4247; Dm: 2.7769
FTSE 350 down 24.4 at 2864.3	**Sterling index** 99.0
FT all share down 21.95 at 2762.73	**Euro** 3 month rate: 3⅞
FT gilts index down 0.50 at 115.98	**US Federal funds rate:** 5(4¾)
Frankfurt down 122.24 at 5270.6	**Gold** down $6.00 at $291.25
Paris down 43.52 at 4201.9	**Oil** Brent February: $12.28
Eurotop 100 down 46.1 at 2862.92	**RPI** 164.4 (February) up 3% on year

Beyond images
Words.
Beyond words

Images.
Beyond both
Neither.

Printless.

Try: cut
: tear
: scratch
: rip

To approx. – (doesn't)

Try: 'speaks for itself':

Try: instructions issued
With the export order –
'How to handle degraded babies':

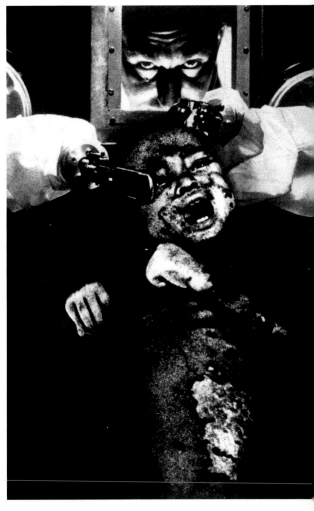

**Speak for others –
Don't.**

Cut a long story short:

Botched telling.
Lip service.
Inchoate (fucked).

Click 1:

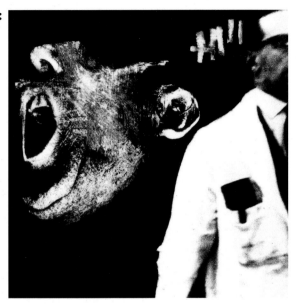

Click 2:

Thinking won't –
My mind's slowed vocabulary
Tries definition:

'Fair [*far*]*n.* periodical market
Often with amusements
Sideshows etc.

Arms–Fair [*aarms far*]*n* .....
....
....'

And fails.

13

In skull
And
Out –

Out of my skull
And
In –

Words
Unpick
Unwords:

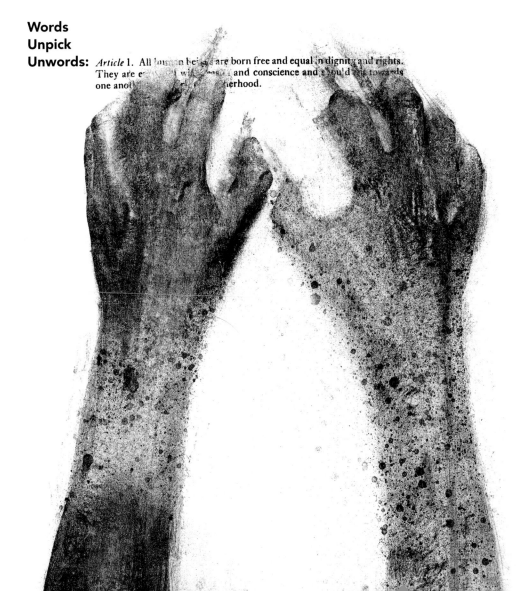

Article 1. All human beings are born free and equal in dignity and rights. They are endowed with reason and conscience and should act towards one another in a spirit of brotherhood.

UNIVERSAL DECLARATION OF HUMAN RIGHTS

Whereas recognition of the inherent dignity and of the equal and inalienable rights of all members of the human family is the foundation of freedom, justice and peace in the world,

Whereas disregard and contempt for human rights have resulted in barbarous acts which have outraged the conscience of mankind, and the advent of a world in which human beings shall enjoy freedom of speech and belief and freedom from fear and want has been proclaimed as the highest aspiration of the common people,

Whereas it is essential, if man is not to be compelled to have recourse, as a last resort, to rebellion against tyranny and oppression, that human rights should be protected by the rule of law,

Whereas it is essential to promote the development of friendly relations between nations,

Whereas the peoples of the United Nations have in the Charter reaffirmed their faith in fundamental human rights, in the dignity and worth of the human person and in the equal rights of men and women and have determined to promote social progress and better standards of life in larger freedom,

Whereas Member States have pledged themselves to achieve, in cooperation with the United Nations, the promotion of universal respect for and observance of human rights and fundamental freedoms,

Whereas a common understanding of these rights and freedoms is of the greatest importance for the full realization of this pledge,

Now, Therefore,

THE GENERAL ASSEMBLY
proclaims

THIS UNIVERSAL DECLARATION OF HUMAN RIGHTS as a common standard of achievement for all peoples and all nations, to the end that every individual and every organ of society, keeping this Declaration constantly in mind, shall strive by teaching and education to promote respect for these rights and freedoms and by progressive measures, national and international, to secure their universal and effective recognition and observance, both among the peoples of Member States themselves and among the peoples of territories under their jurisdiction.

1. *Demands* that all parties and others concerned tree Srebrenica and its surroundings as a safe area which should be free from any armed attack or any othu hostile act

Article 9. No one shall be subjected

ary arrest, detention or exile.

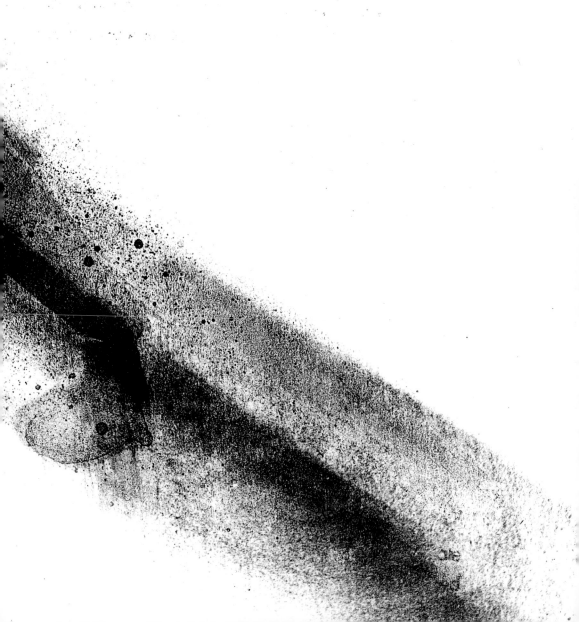

CURRENCY

Article 11. (1) Everyone charged with a penal offence presumed innocent until ... at which he has had all ...

(2) No one shall be held guilty of any penal act or omission which did ... or international law, at the time ... heavier penalty be imposed ... the penal offence was committed ...

Nothing in this Declaration may be interpreted as implying
e, group or person any right to engage in any activity or to perform any
act aimed at the destruction of any of the rights and freedoms.

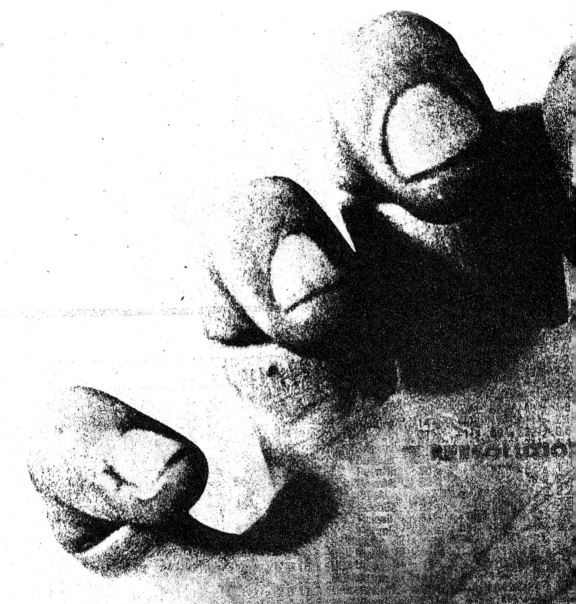

From a gone century
Pitted with ordnance,
I ordnance survey the ordnance:

**Doesn't
Conjure
Up –**

**From carriers
I unpick the bundles,
Click open ring binders,**

**Scatter jottings –
A-X
1-809:**

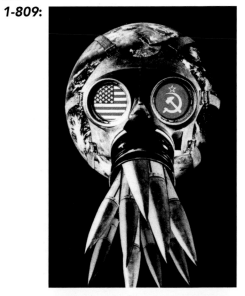

**Jottings take stock
On my skin –
Y-Z:**

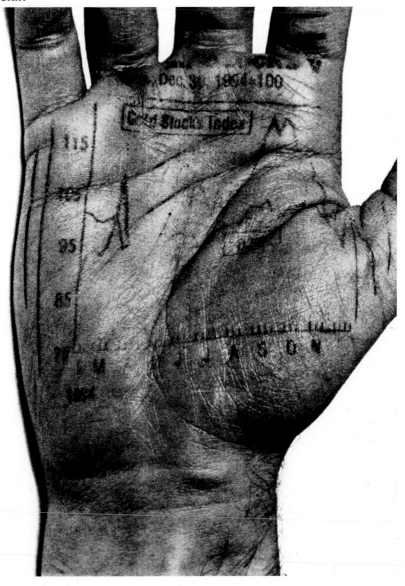

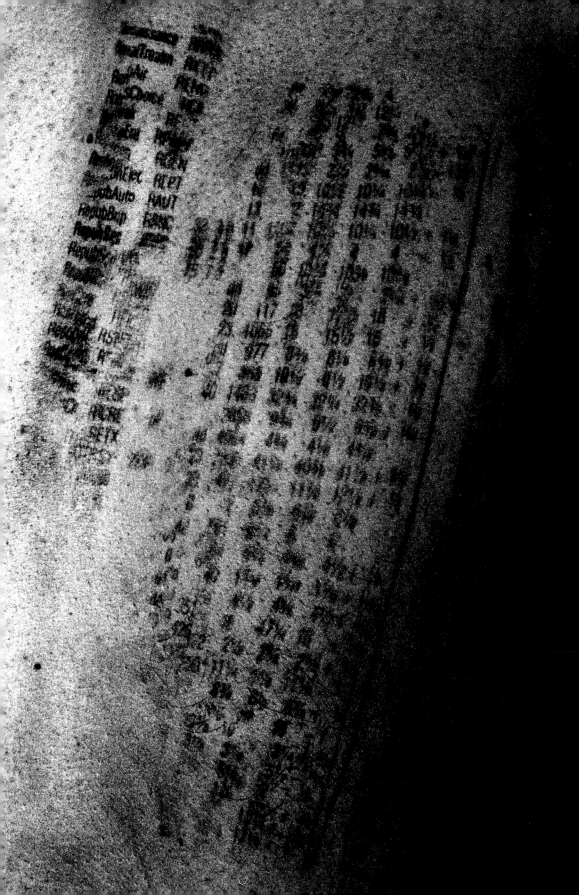

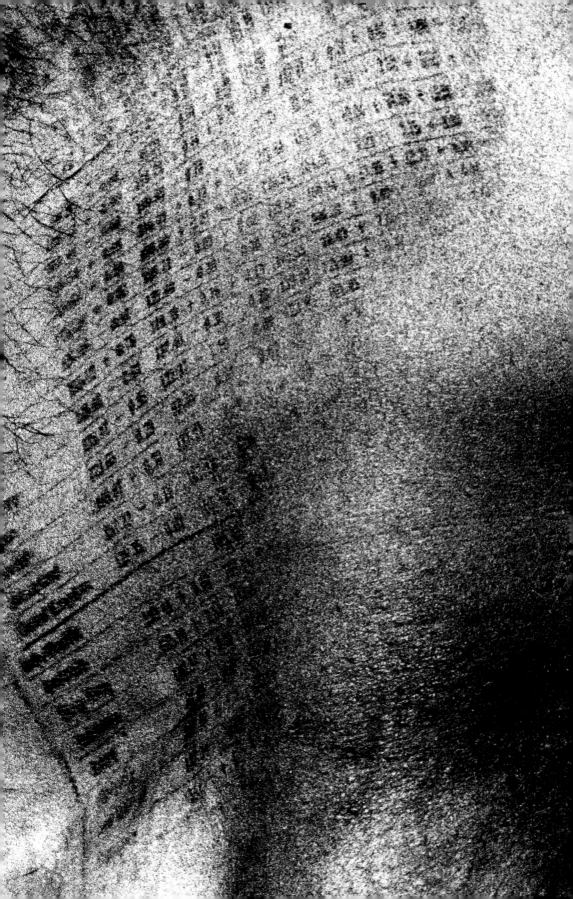

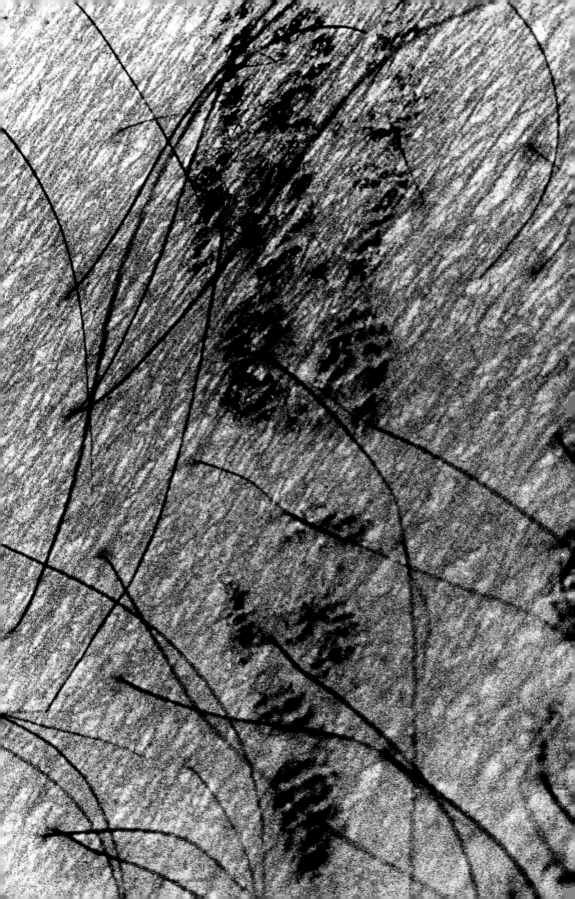

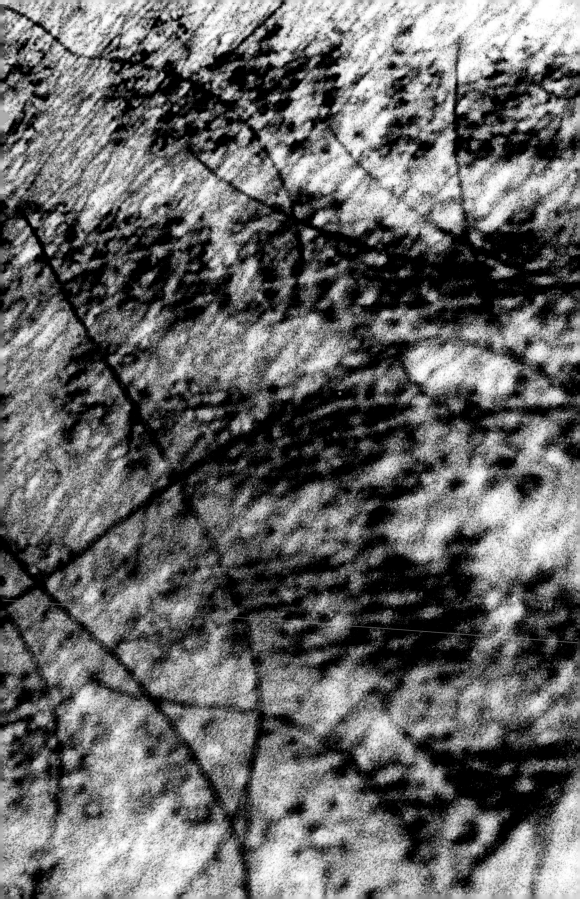

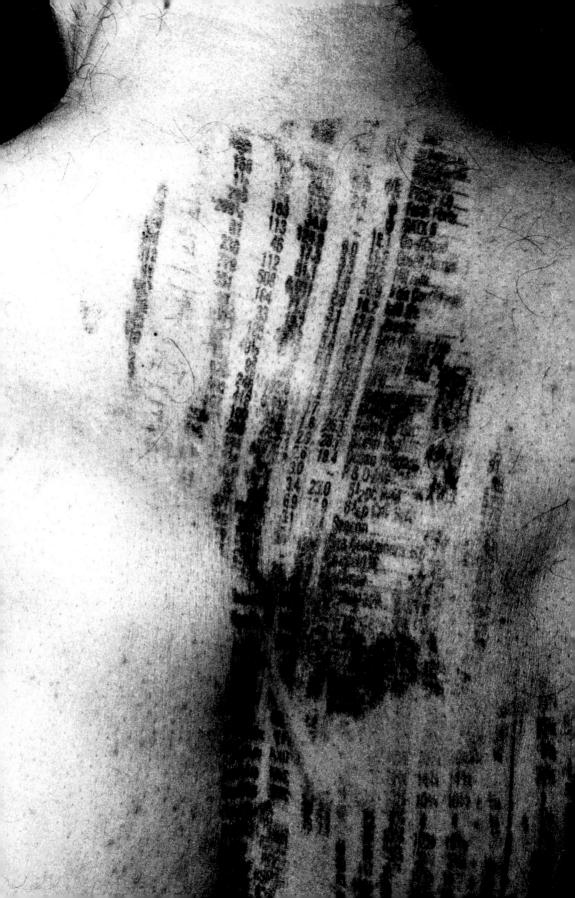

**Infra-red photo cells
Flash the century's
Last photocall.**

**I –
I –
– nothing to declare.**

Click on:

Click off:

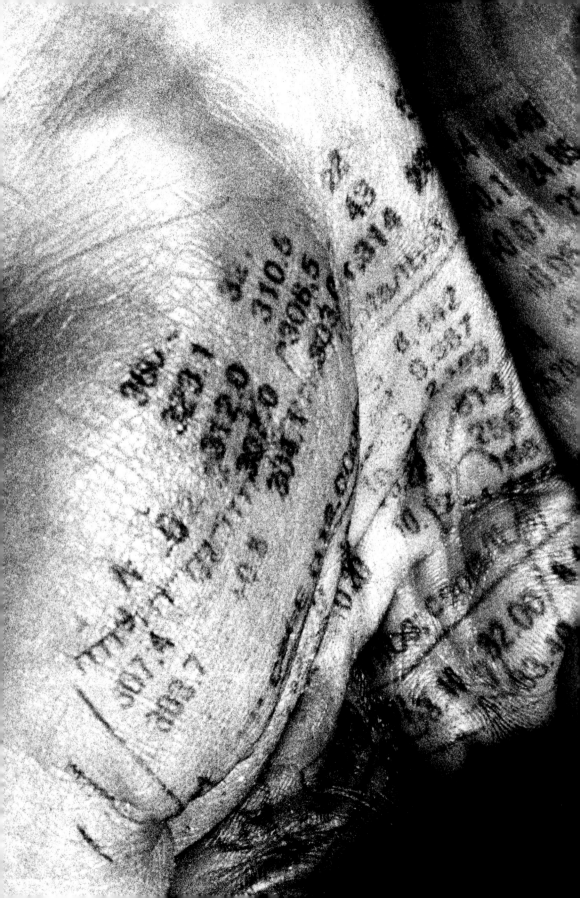

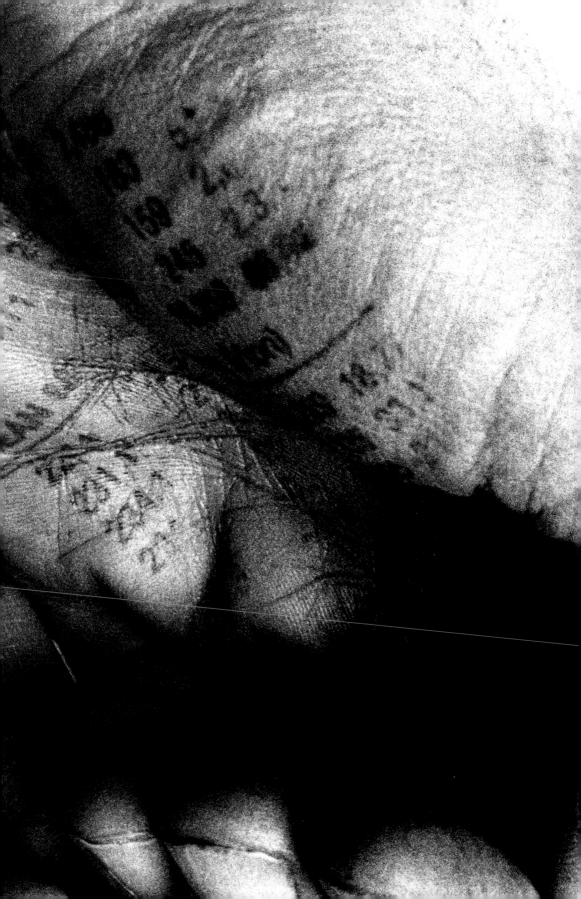

14

Now –
Breaking out from dead centre,
Pushed to the rim,

I crawl over vestiges
Of injured breath
And stutters

Of clothed litter
Thrown
To the dogs.

An international community
Against 'The International Community',
Huddled at the margin.

Their pallets abut,
A raft stained
With traces –

Washed over and over
By *Plc*,
By mines, *Aerospace*, 'Disappeared', gas,

B52's, 'Invisibles', bare wires, *Hawks*, The *IMF*,
Slashed by tank tracks
Their traces remain.

Raft floats on sludge
Against the tide.
Softspeakers hum.

Loudspeakers of State
Bully the air –
No-one listens.

Hands gently cup
A globe
Against 'globalisation',

They eke it out,
Bashed with dreams –
Re:

Re:

Re the:

It's international news,
Unreported
By *News International*'s

Maggots
Feeding on flesh
They buried in muck.

Leaving bones
That rise through the ground
Unstoppable,

Toppling the headstones
Chiselled 'Agenda',
The traces remain.

Now passing through
The nowhere
Of middle,

Where unfixed negatives
Of diners at tables
Fade in the light

From the raft,
Now indelibly stained
By the traces of another.

These traces hold –
They are loss adjusters,
Cleaving back

Their bodies
From the butcher's block
Where all is unsaid and done.

In their floating lab,
Ear to the ground,
They R and D the possible –

Blueprinting conversion,
Their voices
Mime blanks to the censor.

While hardware,
Chewed out of shape
Is spat

into shape.

These mouths
That are chewing
Are the mouths

That were gagged.
Forming language to index
An archive of anger

Whispered
On and on
Without let up.

They lip-read the traces,
Resist through numbers,
Morph a count-down

From metal.
Invent
In reverse: 10   9   8   7   6   5   4   3   2   1   0

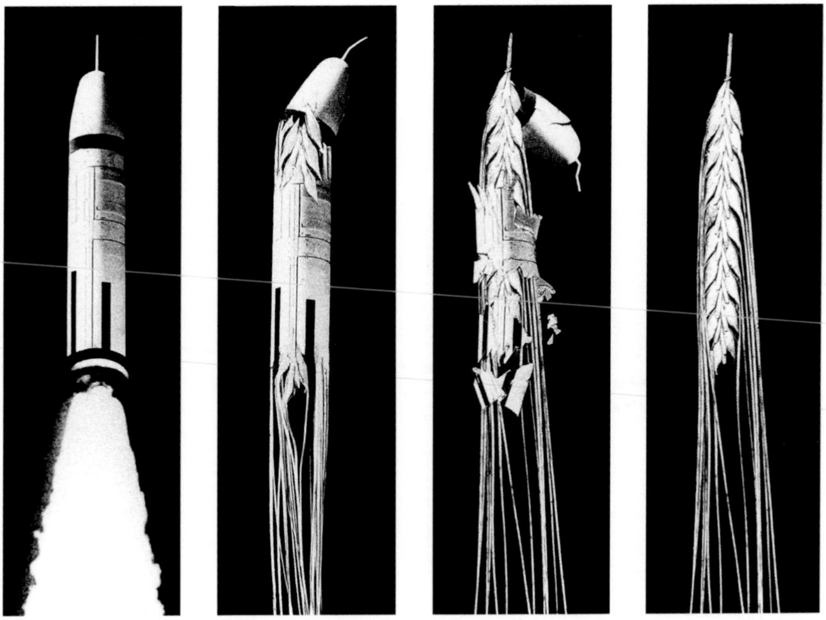

In the shape
Of things
To go:

Omit:

Omit:

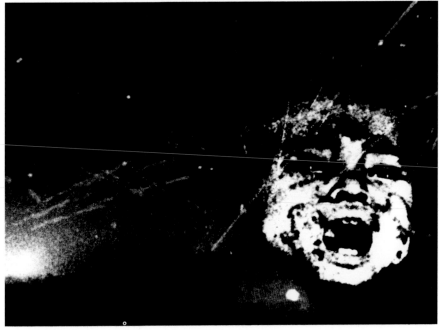

Omit:

Speaking out from the O,
Traces stain traces –
Traces endure –

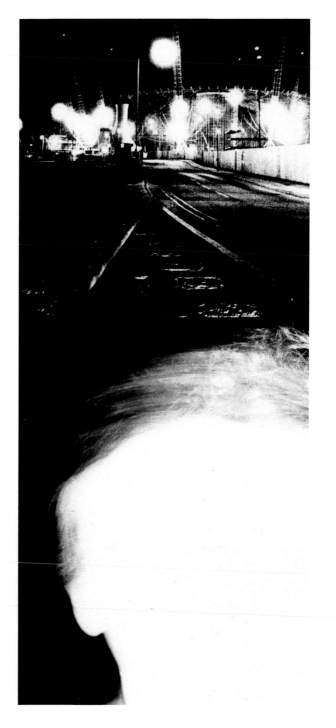

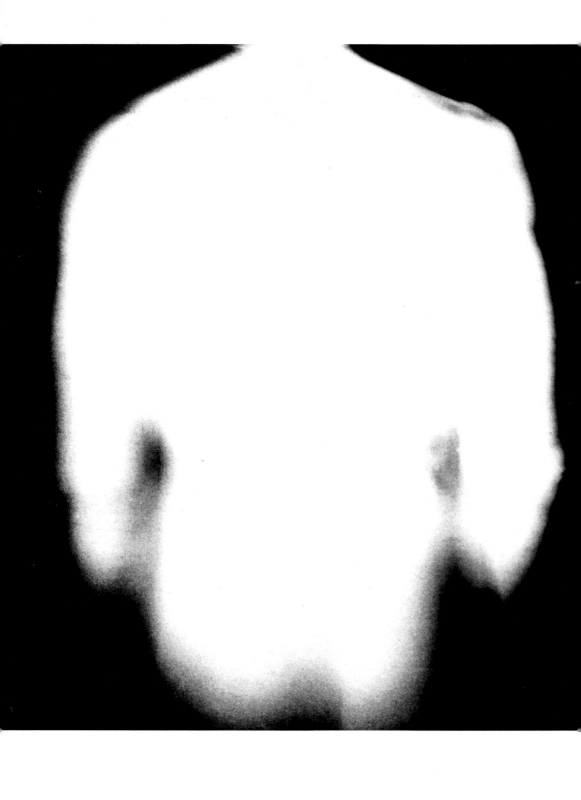

An inventory voiced,
Fuelled by a back-fired propellant
Of mouth beyond muzzle,

Speech beyond lip service,
Beyond slash and burn.
A future not Futures.

The mouths
That speak,
Speak – 'Fragile':

Flick the damn switch.
Keep vision on.
Sound on.

Quit the artist's impression.
Listen.
The silenced

Speak:

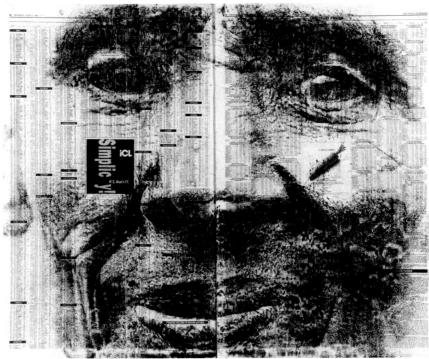

Speak:

Speak:

Speak:

Speak:

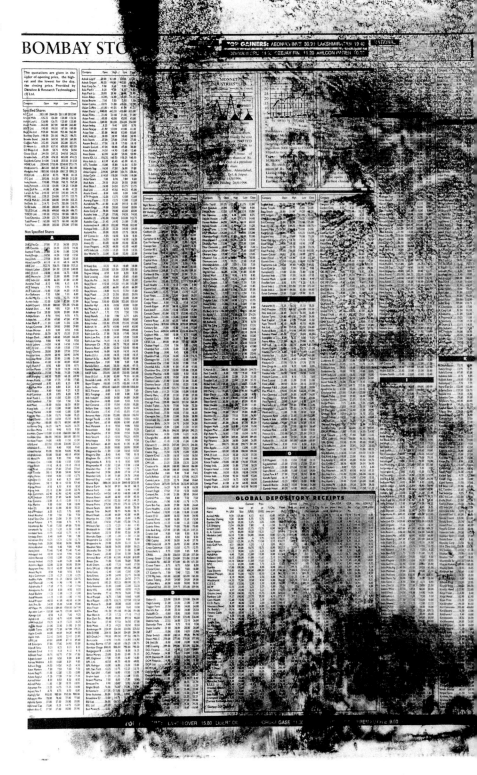

Speak:

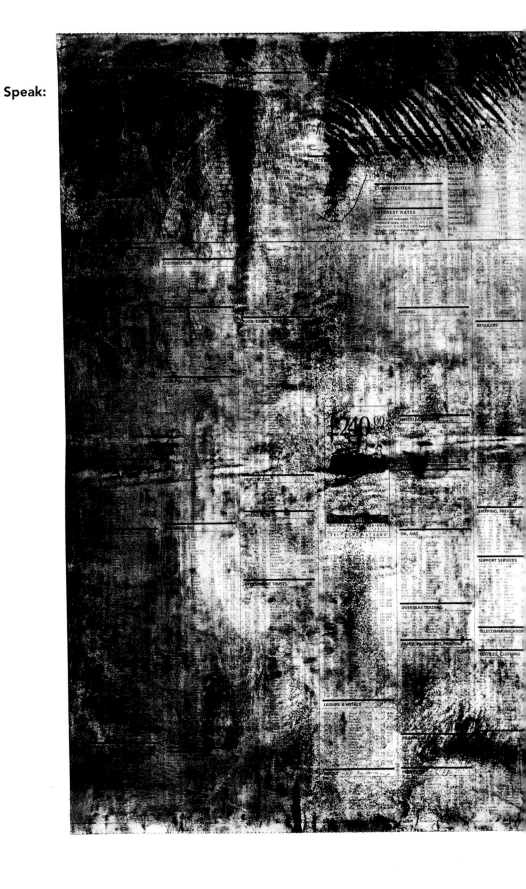

d safety bodies failing public, claims expert

Anti BSE ...cost ...£...m

UNIT TRUSTS

INSURANCE BONDS

Speak:

Auslandsbörsen   Devisenmarkt   Warenmärkte

Amerika   Asien / Australien

Leichtere Tendenz folgt einer freundlichen Eröffnung   Knapp behauptete Kurse in Tokio

Speak:

Scheuring consortium video disk

Philips en Sony samen
verder na onenigheid

AEX vliegt omh

Wall Street euforis

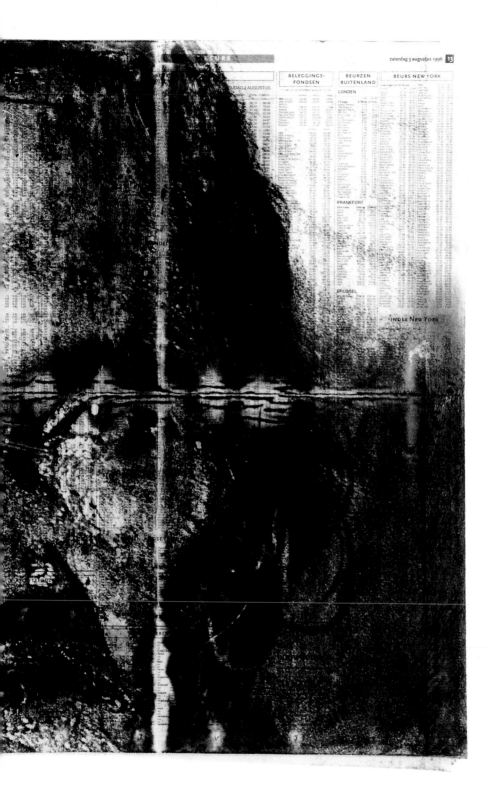

BELEGGINGS-
FONDSEN

BEURZEN
BUITENLAND

BEURS NEW YORK

LONDEN

FRANKFORT

BRUSSEL

INDEX NEW YORK

Speak:

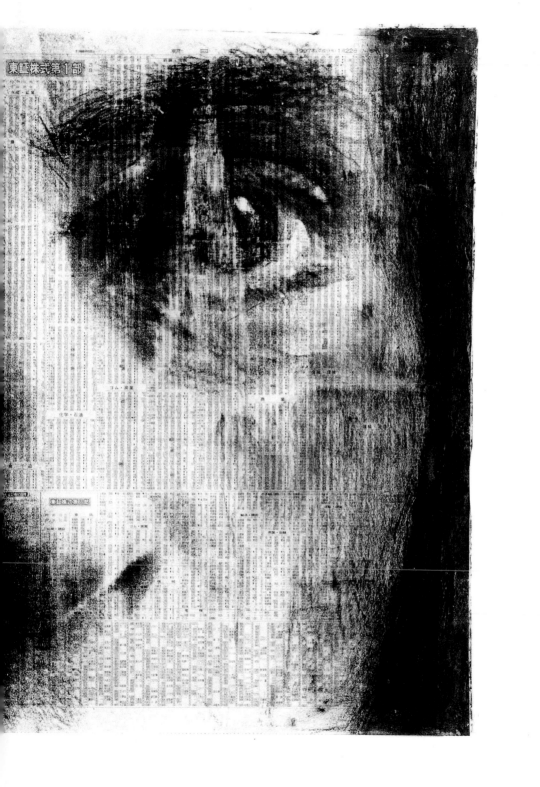

Speak:

Speak:

Firm end to the week

Speak:

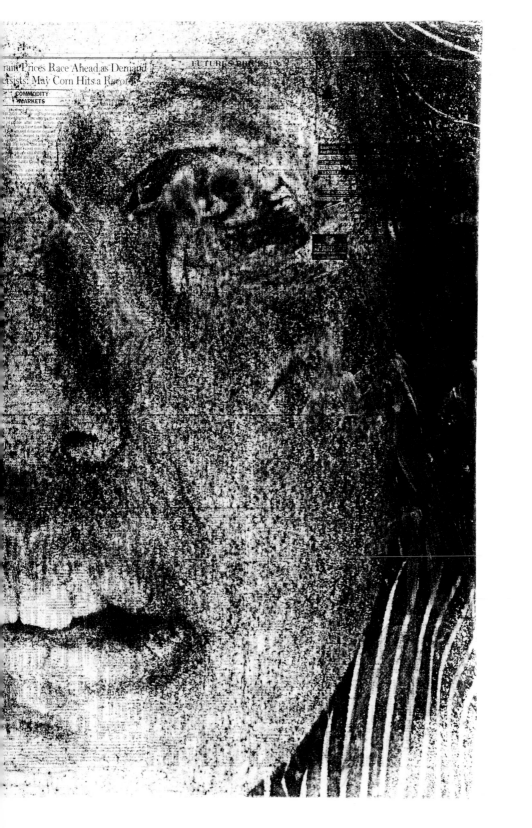

Speak:

Speak:

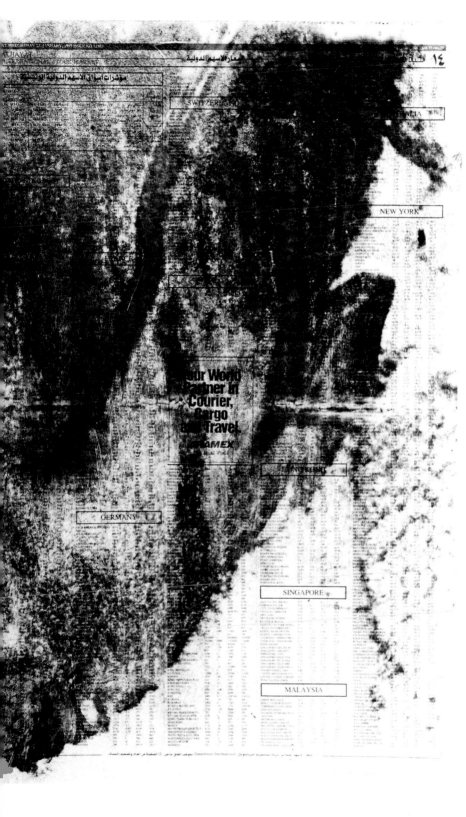

Speak:

NEW YORK STOCK EXCHANGE TRANSACTIONS

Continued From Preceding Page

-L-L-L-

-N-N-N-

-M-M-M-

-O-O-O-

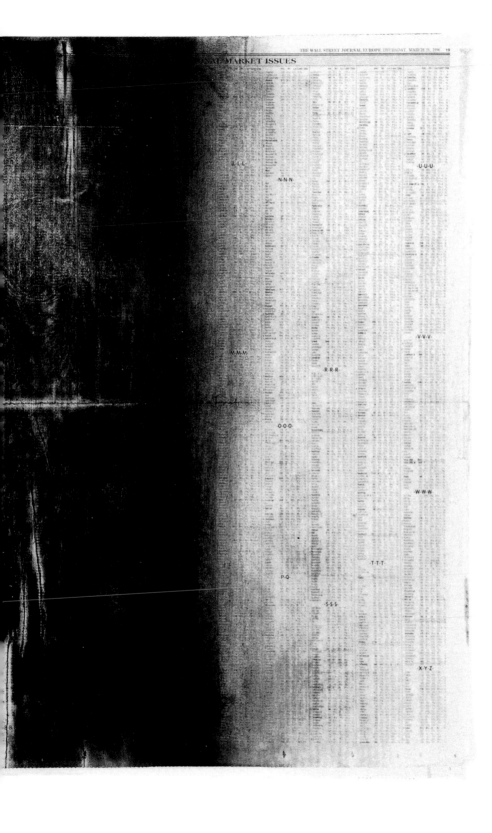

Speak:

...den sets bench mark | New lease
for German expansion ... of life for

... property well sold

Riding ... on
a roller coaster bet

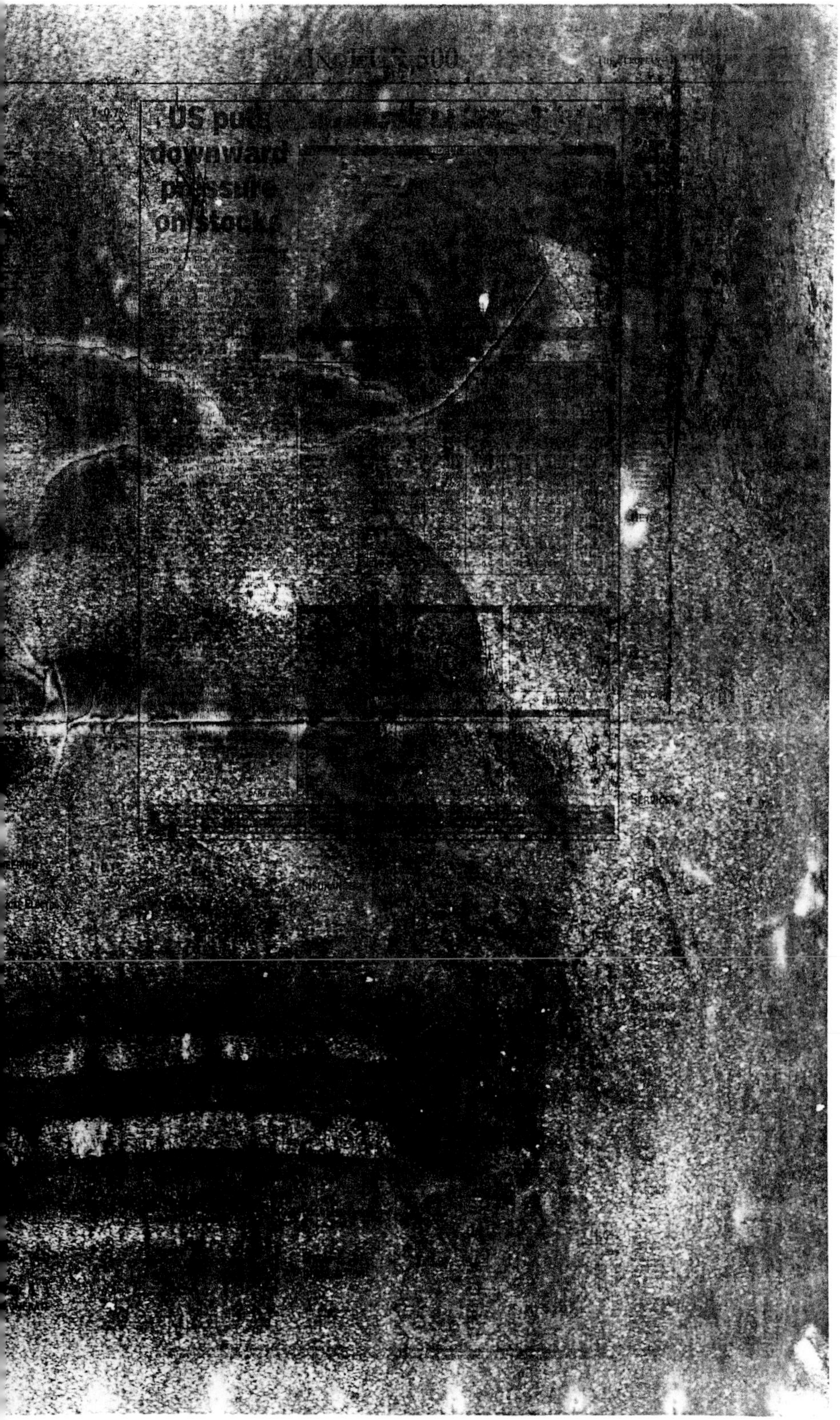

US push
downward
pressure
on stocks

Speak:

NYSE

Friday's 4 p.m. Close

Nationwide prices, not reflecting late trades elsewhere
The Associated Press

U.S. Chip Accord With Japanese Will Meet With EU Opposition

Japanese Order 22 Boeing Jets

TOKYO — Two Japanese trading companies said Friday that they had ordered 22 Boeing passenger airplanes in a deal worth $1.1 billion.

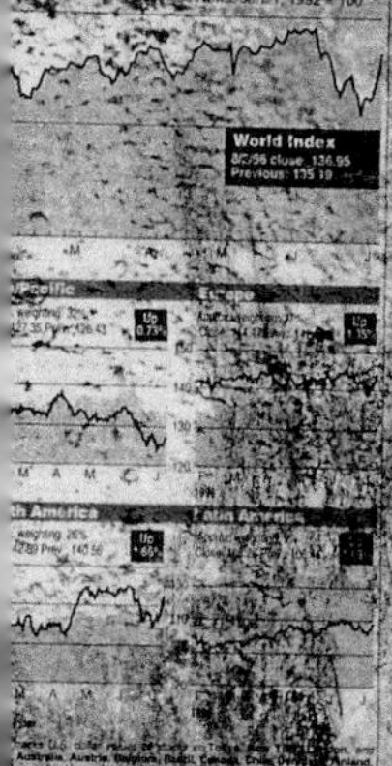

Osaka-based Itochu Corp, one of Japan's top five general traders, will spend $600 million to purchase 12 of the B737-800 aircraft, said a company spokesman. Take-hiko Kigura.

Kanematsu Corp., based in Tokyo, bought 10 of the jets for $500 million, a company spokesman said.

The company will form a leasing company with DATX Capital of the United States and one other U.S. company.

The two spokesmen said most of the planes that had been purchased would be leased abroad.

The first delivery of the B737-800, which seats 189 people, is expected in April, with the rest being handed over by 2000, they said.

Mr. Kigura added, however, that two of the jets were bought on option, meaning that the orders for those aircraft could be cancelled later.

He said some of the aircraft purchased by Itochu would be sold.

The Kanematsu spokesman said the two orders were unrelated.

Japan's leading business daily, the Nihon Keizai Shimbun, said the purchases symbolized improved prospects for the aircraft leasing business, which has been in the doldrums.

Itochu's wholly-owned subsidiary, Itochu AirLease (Europe) Ltd., which will execute the order, will sell four of the aircraft and lease six to Air España SA, a Spanish airline company.

Itochu will look for other operators to lease the remaining two planes, the spokesman said. *(AP, Reuters, Knight-Ridder)*

■ **Eurocopter Wins Saudi Contract**

Eurocopter, a helicopter maker controlled by Aérospatiale of France and Daimler-Benz Aerospace AG, said it has won a contract to supply Saudi Arabia with 12 combat helicopters, shutting out U.S. rivals Sikorsky and McDonnell Douglas Corp., Bloomberg Business News reported Friday from Paris.

Under the contract, which analysts gauge to be worth about 3 billion francs ($600 million), Eurocopter will provide the country with 12 Cougar Mark II search and rescue helicopters, as well as maintenance and logistical support.

It's welcome news for a company that's been through a rough patch," said Jacques de Greling, an analyst at Transboursie.

The deal reaffirms the four-year-old, money-losing Eurocopter's viability just one year after McDonnell shut it out of a $4.4 billion combat helicopter order from Britain and an $830 million contract from the Dutch government.

"It's an important contract for us," said Eurocopter spokesman, Jean-Louis Espes. "Pursuing our export markets is particularly important."

With defense budgets shrinking in France and Germany as part of the effort to trim deficits before European monetary union, such companies as Eurocopter depend more on exports.

For Eurocopter, which had sales of 9.3 billion francs and a total of 7.2 billion francs in orders on its books at the end of 1995, the contract fleshes out what already looks to be a promising year. In February, the company won an order from Spain for 15 Cougar Mark I's. In May, it agreed to jointly build 80 Ecureuil helicopters with Industria Aeronautique Roumaine of Romania.

The size and technological sophistication of the helicopters in the Saudi deal adds to the contract's cachet, Eurocopter said.

Is the Big Board Better? AOL Thinks So

By David S. Hilzenrath and Brett D. Fromson
Washington Post Service

When America Online Inc. announced that it would abandon the Nasdaq stock market in favor of the New York Stock Exchange, it had shone a spotlight on one of the business world's fiercest rivalries.

The two exchanges vie to host the trading of shares in top companies, but still the debate rages. What difference does it really make where a company's stock is listed?

America Online, the world's largest on-line services provider, said Thursday a move to the Big Board offered the potential to find out faster who is buying and selling its stock, to get better pricing for investors, to gain greater exposure to an international market and to enjoy less trading volatility.

"Clearly in our eyes, the New York Stock Exchange got the gold medal, here," said Richard E. Hanlon, the company's vice president of investor relations.

But other companies disagree.

"We just don't see why it's any better than Nasdaq," said James Jarrett, vice president of investor relations at Intel Corp., the computer chipmaker with $16.2 billion in sales last year. Intel has resisted overtures from the NYSE and is the second largest company on Nasdaq. "The investors don't seem to care," he said. "It just doesn't come up."

The two markets operate in fundamentally different ways. In New York, all trades converge on a trading floor where a "specialist" is appointed for each company to coordinate orders delivered by floor brokers and the much larger volume that comes in electronically. Nasdaq has no trading floor and no specialist. Competing securities dealers exchange buy and sell offers over a computer network and complete their trades in cyberspace. America Online's controversial stay was particularly conspicuous because Nasdaq has promoted itself as the place for fast-growing high-tech companies.

Marc Beauchamp, a Nasdaq spokesman, said Thursday: "I think it's god to do more with what's going on at America Online than it does with what's going on at Nasdaq."

America Online's stock has lost more than half its value since early May.

America Online expects the "spreads" — between prices offered by buyers and sellers could be narrower on the NYSE, making the stock more appealing to investors because each trade would not come with such a big markup.

Mr. Beauchamp said that America Online shares had been trading recently in increments of one-eighth, just as they would on the NYSE. He attributed the wide spreads in AOL shares during May and June to the big fall the stock took after America Online announced poor earnings.

■ **CompuServe Ends Europe Talks**

CompuServe Corp said Friday it had ended talks with Europe Online SA on taking a stake in the troubled on-line information service, Bloomberg Business News reported from Columbus, Ohio.

"Terms could not be reached," CompuServe said without providing details. Europe Online won court protection from creditors last month.

ECONOMIC SCENE

Investors Watch Thai Squeeze Play

By Kevin Murphy

[Column of text largely illegible]

See **THAILAND, Page 13**

Petersen Magazines Said to Attract Major Bids

By Robin Pogrebin
New York Times Service

NEW YORK — Several prominent magazine companies are bidding to buy Petersen Publishing Co., which publishes such established titles as Hot Rod, Motor Trend, Guns & Ammo and Sassy, according to sources close to the negotiations.

Among those said to be interested in the property are K-III Communications, a unit of Kohlberg Kravis Roberts & Co.

that publishes magazines such as New York and Soap Opera Digest; Times Mirror Co., which, along with its news papers, publishes 11 special-interest magazines such as Outdoor Life and Popular Science; Morteiner Zuckerman, who owns U.S. News & World Report and The Atlantic Monthly, as well as The Daily News in New York; Claeys Bahrenburg, former president of Hearst Magazines; and American Media Inc., which publishes The National Enquirer and The Star.

Petersen is expected to sell for between $375 million and $475 million, according to one prospective buyer.

Goldman, Sachs & Co. is handling the sale, which is expected to be completed within the next two weeks.

Robert Petersen, the chairman and founder of Petersen Publishing, started Hot Rod magazine in 1947. Since then the company has amassed some 27 regular monthly magazines and 57 that are published sporadically, and about 45 million adult readers.

CURRENCY & INTEREST RATES

Libid-Libor Rates

Speak:

Speak:

Speak:

Money Market
Trust Funds

Money Market
Bank Accounts

Speak:

Speak:

,

Speak:

Speak:

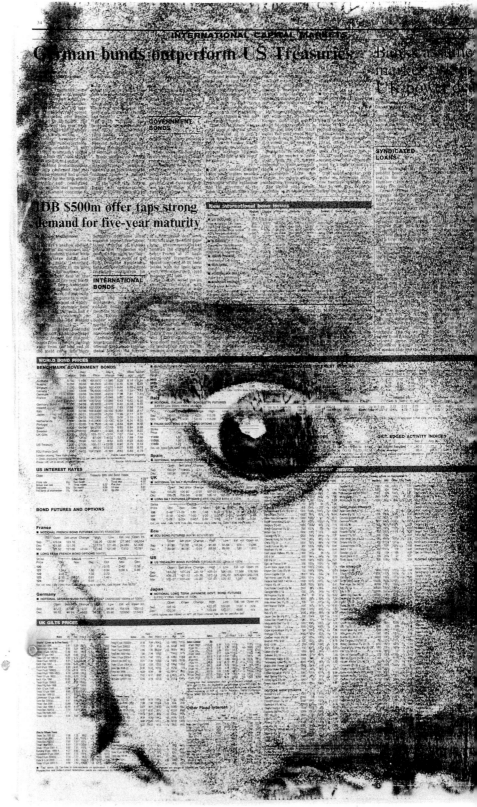

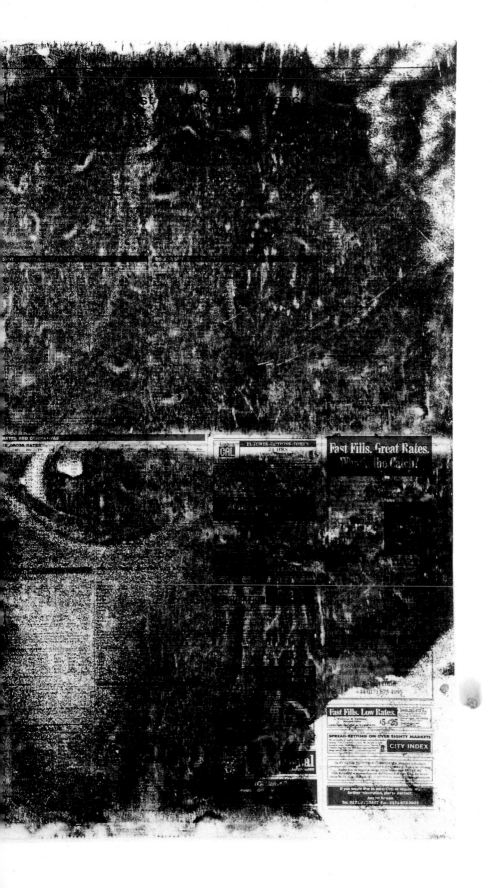

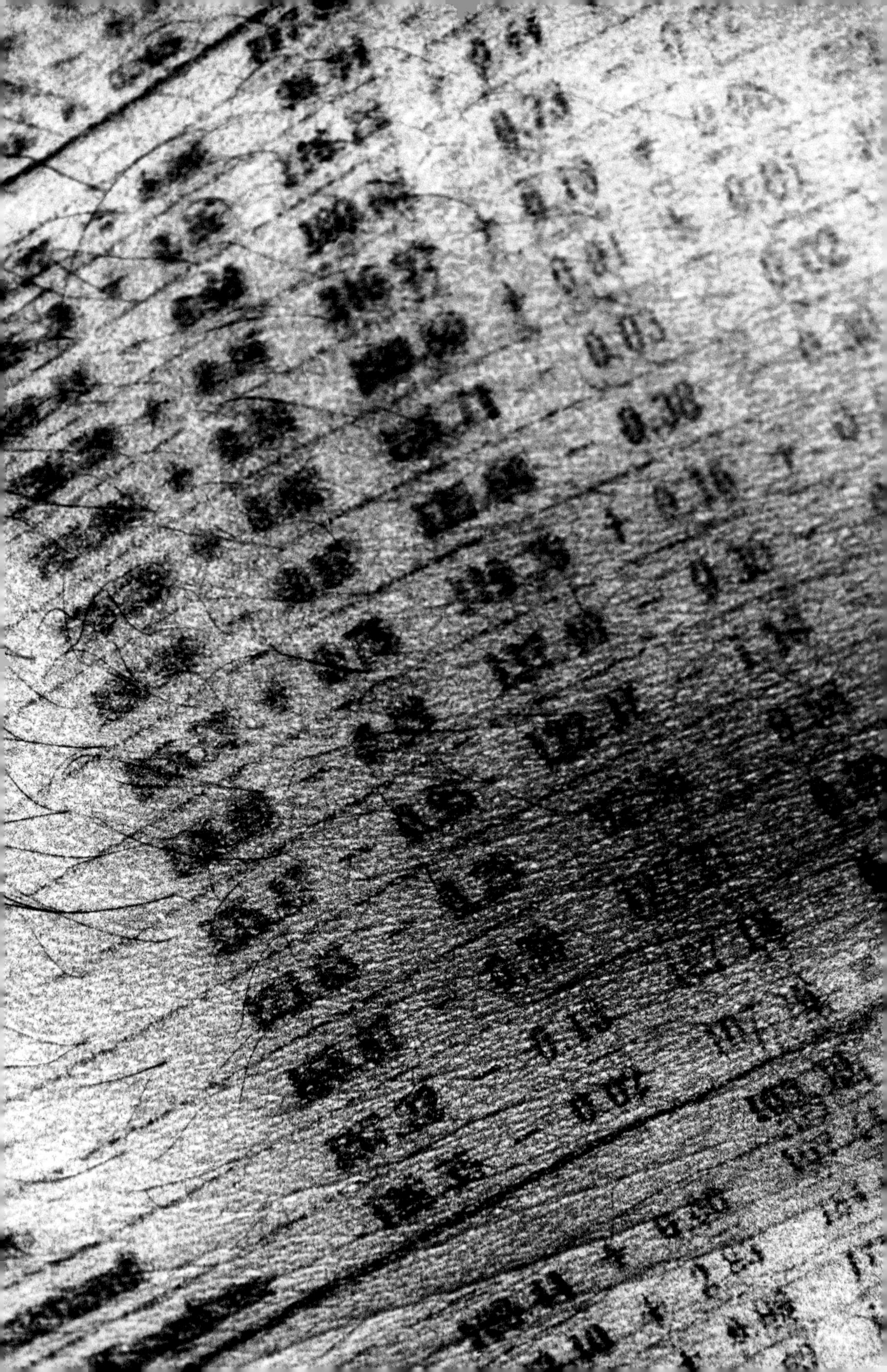